Fighting the Battles Within

Discover God's Plan for Overcoming the Strongholds,
Walls, and Giants in Your Life

Bishop Anthony T. Pelt

Sermon To Book
www.sermontobook.com

Fighting the Battles Within / Anthony T. Pelt
ISBN: 978-1-945793-88-2

To my "BabyDoll" Millicent—
Thank you for pushing me into purpose.

Imani, Ty, and Hope—
Love you much.

Hardy and Norma Pelt—
Thank you for being Holy Ghost-filled parents.

All evangelists, like Betty Haynie, Willie Cooper, and Carolyn Menendez—
Thank you for preaching to me, praying for me, and teaching me that spiritual warfare is real.

House of Radiant and Florida-Cocoa—
Let's stay Radiant and Cocoa strong!

CONTENTS

Fight the Good Fight

But without faith it is impossible to please Him, for he who comes to God must believe that He is, and that He is a rewarder of those who diligently seek Him.

—Hebrews 11:6

Of all the things worth fighting for—your integrity, your marriage, your children—your faith is one of the most important. Without faith, after all, it is impossible to please God (Hebrews 11:6).

I'm not talking about fighting for the right to share your faith publicly, though that's important, too. Rather, I'm talking about fighting spiritual battles against Satan, the enemy of your soul, and the strongholds he seeks to introduce into your life.

Everyone has had someone or something in their lives they don't want to confront, allowing it to wreak havoc instead of dealing with it. Whether it's a personal issue, a family issue, or a spiritual issue, you cannot overcome it unless you engage it.

Too often, these issues—these strongholds we'd prefer not to confront—keep us from the fullness of life that God wants for us. Satan doesn't want you to have what God wants you to have (John 10:10). To get what God wants you to have, you will need to fight for it. The good news is that God has authorized you to do battle. And because He has authorized you to do battle, you need to do battle His way, not your way.

It's important to remember that these battles are not against other people—they're against the spiritual realm (Ephesians 6:12). Too often, strongholds of Satan keep you from the fullness of life. (John 10:10). God wants you to fight—especially when it involves the realm of darkness (1 Timothy 6:12). Remember, you aren't fighting other people, but shrewd spirits who want to rob you of your hope and your faith. This means that you must learn to fight God's way.

Sometimes, you'll fight without the support of other people. As a teenager, David the shepherd—and future king of Israel—took on the Philistine giant, Goliath, one-on-one. (1 Samuel 17). Beating all the odds, David felled Goliath with just one stone and then cut off Goliath's head with Goliath's own sword and won the victory for Israel. This is a magnificent story, and we all wish we had the faith of David in battle!

But often, you will need others' help to succeed. I am reminded of one point in the Israelites' journey through the desert (Exodus 17:9–13). The Amalekites attacked them mercilessly while they camped at Rephidim. So, Moses told Joshua to take some men and fight off the Amalekites while Moses stood on the top of the hill with the staff of God in his hands. So the next day, Moses, Aaron, and Hur stood on a hill watching the battle below. As long as Moses held up the staff, the Israelites prevailed.

Now if you have ever held anything high above your head, you know that after a while, it gets *really* hard. But if Moses lowered his hands, the Amalekites began to win. When Moses became fatigued, Aaron and Hur sat him down on a rock and they stood on each side of him to help hold up his arms. Joshua won, and the Amalekites were routed (Exodus 17:11–12). This is a picture of a team effort. Moses helped Joshua; Aaron and Hur helped Moses; and, of course, God helped them all.

It doesn't matter if you are alone or with others; God will always be by your side and on your side.

Think about it. Is it possible that you have allowed too many battles to go unfought for too long? Are there strongholds in your life you need to confront and tear down? Do you want to know what victory in Christ feels like?

These things I have spoken to you, that in Me you may have peace. In the world you will have tribulation; but be of good cheer, I have overcome the world.
—John 16:33

Strongholds are tricky to detect and a challenge to overcome. But remember, Jesus has overcome the world and has sent the Holy Spirit to give us discernment.

In this book, you'll discover what the Bible has to say about fighting these spiritual battles and learn how to fight

God's way. Additionally, workbook sections at the end of each chapter will guide you in personalizing and retaining the truths that will lead you to victory.

Let's prepare for battle!

Part One: Strongholds

CHAPTER ONE

What Is a Stronghold?

For though we walk in the flesh, we do not war according to the flesh. For the weapons of our warfare are not carnal but mighty in God for pulling down strongholds, casting down arguments and every high thing that exalts itself against the knowledge of God, bringing every thought into captivity to the obedience of Christ, and being ready to punish all disobedience when your obedience is fulfilled.
—2 Corinthians 10:3–6

In 2 Corinthians 10:4, the word for *stronghold* is used in a unique way compared to other usages of the word in Scripture. Stronghold is typically used to signify a safe place, or even God Himself, but the usage here indicates something that is built based on a certain false belief you have.

The original Greek word used for *stronghold* in 2 Corinthians 10:4 is *ochyrōma,* which means "a castle, stronghold, fortress, fastness; anything on which one relies; *the arguments and reasonings by which a disputant endeavors to fortify his opinion and defend it against his opponent.*"[1] A stronghold is like a wall protecting a lie of the enemy in your mind. It is a metaphor for fleshly confidence in anything other than the mind of God. A stronghold clouds your perception and keeps you from recognizing truth. It also distorts the present with issues from the past.

If the enemy keeps you focused on issues ungrounded in biblical truth, he can distract you from doing what God wants and from being effective in your Christian walk. But the good news is that God gives you weapons to tear down these strongholds.

The concept of strongholds is considered somewhat archaic in some Christian circles these days. Many Christians may shirk the idea of "tearing down strongholds" because some believers may go overboard and approach spiritual battles like mythical ghost busters. They treat every stronghold as something caused by an ungodly spirit living in you—a spirit of fear, a spirit of lust, and so forth. The truth is that sometimes, a stronghold is just your own doing. You may be clinging to false perceptions built up over time, protecting them and afraid of what exposing them may do.

Unfortunately, that can swing the pendulum in the other direction. When you realize a stronghold isn't necessarily caused by an ungodly spirit but may just be a personal issue, you may minimize the spiritual aspect of the problem. Either way, the enemy wins. He knows that there are two competing views on strongholds. One overstresses the spiritual, and the other dismisses it. Satan uses both perspectives against you.

So, the debate rages in your mind—on the one hand, a spirit may be tormenting you, but on the other hand, you may be intentionally defending a lie to protect yourself. Until *"Gotcha!"* That's the subtlety of a stronghold—you may not know you're locked up until you can't get out.

As you continue in your study of strongholds and the many ways they can affect you, always remember that you are not just a physical being with a personal history. You are also a spiritual being affected by the spiritual climate around you. Satan knows that if you ever take the spiritual realm seriously, your natural self is going to change. The last thing he wants to see is an obedient and happy child of God. If you are armed with knowledge about the strongholds that can affect you, you will be better equipped to rely on God to overcome them.

Strongholds Affecting Faith

Unfortunately, many of the strongholds that believers face are ones that are rooted in the context of the church. These strongholds ultimately affect your faith negatively and hinder the overall growth of the church. They can be just as dangerous—if not more so—as the temptations lurking in the secular world.

Stronghold of Religion

A common stronghold that affects many believers, is a stronghold of religion. The phrase *stronghold of religion* may sound like a contradiction in terms but let me explain. You see, people today often want salvation without the accompanying transformation or the necessary sacrifice. They want to be saved the way they want to be saved, not the way the Bible says to be saved. Have you ever heard people talk about personal salvation and church affairs "back in the day?" Despite the stringent practices of the previous generation, most folks agree that church culture used to better reflect the Bible than the way we do things now.

People don't want to go back to the "old ways" and risk making some of the same mistakes, yet are dissatisfied with current trends, so they end up having a stronghold of religion. Disdain for the way things are continues to fester, while they can't fully commit to any changes to increase their growth or the spreading of the gospel. Who benefits from that?

Strongholds Surrounding Preachers

Some have strongholds surrounding preachers. At some point in their lives, a preacher said or did something that had a negative effect on them. This evoked certain ways of thinking about all preachers and gave the enemy an entry point to start building up a stronghold.

The person thinks they are protecting themselves from being hurt this way again. The enemy has convinced this person that they are building up a place of safety, but it's really a place of imprisonment.

Part of my job as a preacher is to live in such a way that God can show these people that not all preachers are like the one who hurt them. But only God can touch their minds to pull down that stronghold. They must use the weapons of warfare that God has given them and fight.

Strongholds Against the Bible

Some have a stronghold against reading the Bible regularly. They are convinced that if it's read in church, they don't need to read it for themselves. The truth of the matter is that you aren't likely to apply the scriptures you hear in church if reading the Word is not a regular aspect of your lifestyle. You might get a little bit out of it, but for the most part, you won't truly benefit from the wisdom and knowledge in Scripture until you pursue it for yourself. What does the Bible have to say about that? It's dangerous.

My people are destroyed for lack of knowledge. Because you have rejected knowledge, I also will reject you from being priest for Me; Because you have forgotten the law of your God, I also will forget your children.
—Hosea 4:6

God's people are not destroyed for lack of preaching or lack of singing—they are destroyed for lack of knowledge. As a result, we have people in the church who are fleshly, who are ruled by their emotions rather than by the Almighty God. And they don't even know the difference.

These strongholds which affect the faith are dangerous, but they aren't the only ones a Christian needs to be on guard against.

Other Strongholds

Strongholds related to the foundations of our faith—religion, pastors, reading the Bible—are favorites of the enemy, but you can have a stronghold in any area of your life.

Strongholds Against Risk

One such example is the risk-averse mindset. Some people think that trying to change their unfavorable circumstances will only lead to failure and a situation even worse than the present. They're afraid to leave a dead-end job—or to find a job at all—because of the risk involved. In this case, you are trapped if you do and trapped if you don't. What a futile way to live.

> *And my God shall supply all your need according to His riches in glory by Christ Jesus.*
> **—Philippians 4:19**

In the Book of Ruth, the Bible gives us a prime example of godly risk-taking. Naomi was leaving Moab for Israel. She told her widowed daughters-in-law to stay in Moab where they might have a chance for remarriage and a new life. Orpah did. But Ruth loved Naomi and she especially loved Naomi's God, whom she had come to trust (Ruth 1:6–17).

Ruth tells Naomi, "Entreat me not to leave you, or to turn back from following after you; for wherever you go,

I will go; and wherever you lodge, I will lodge; your people shall be my people, and your God, my God. Where you die, I will die, and there will I be buried. The LORD do so to me, and more also, if anything but death parts you and me" (Ruth 1:16–17). The words are familiar to us—written on napkins, banners, songs, announcements, and countless other miscellany by newlyweds who share her sentiments.

But think about it. Ruth was giving up life as she had known it in Moab. She was a widow, with no personal resources. Naomi was old and poor and really had no idea how she would survive when she returned to her homeland. And Naomi was depressed, very depressed. She felt abandoned by God after losing her husband and two sons in this foreign land. Not a very hopeful picture for a young woman like Ruth, an unwelcome foreigner from a hated rival nation.

This was not a romantic adventure for Ruth, but a step of radical faith and trust in God. If you read the end of the story (Ruth 4:13–18), you see that the Lord blessed Ruth beyond her wildest dreams. But first she had to take a risk and trust Him.

Are you ready to trust Him? Let's say, for instance, that you have a job with low pay, long hours, unsafe conditions, and an abusive boss. You hate it, but you're afraid to quit because then you won't have any job and you might not find another. If you never try, you can't fail, right? Sounds like a destructive stronghold.

Now add in the God factor: since God will supply all your needs, you can look for a job and be confident that He'll provide. Remember Ruth. You can move out of your fear and hopelessness into the provision of God. This doesn't necessarily mean you'll move to the fanciest house in the richest neighborhood, but you don't have to live out your life in a box on the side of the road, either. The true reward is growing in your relationship with God and believing in His love for you. That's a God-focused mindset.

Strongholds of Money

The risk-averse mindset isn't the only money-related stronghold. Some people have a love of money. They can't get enough of it. Money is not a bad thing in and of itself, but the love of money is a very different story:

> *For the love of money is a root of all kinds of evil, for which some have strayed from the faith in their greediness, and pierced themselves through with many sorrows.*
> **—1 Timothy 6:10**

You appreciate money for what it can do for you and your loved ones, but money doesn't solve every problem. Remember, God will supply all your needs. Loving money more than you love God and more than you love people creates more problems than it will ever solve—for you and for others. When you love money to the point that you think you can't live without it, it has become a stronghold and you need to break up with it.

These strongholds may be built up by you or by the Satan, but either way, when dealing with the strongholds at play in your life, you must remember you have an adversary.

You Have an Adversary

As the Father loved Me, I also have loved you; abide in My love. If you keep My commandments, you will abide in My love, just as I have kept My Father's commandments and abide in His love.

—John 15:9–10

Satan is your enemy based on the sheer fact that God loves you. The sooner you understand this, the better. It will explain many of your struggles in this life. Satan operates in both the physical and the spiritual realms. He can do things in the spiritual realm to prevent you from being effective in the physical realm!

Likewise, he can mess up the physical realm to prevent you from being effective in the spiritual realm. He preys on your flesh to magnify the cares of the world and to keep you from fully embracing the gospel (Matthew 13:18–23). And he constantly tries to build strongholds in your mind to hide behind.

Though God has imposed certain restrictions on Satan, Satan doesn't play fair. He is a created being, a spirit who can only operate in time and space. He must use humans to do his bidding because he is powerless to build or invent anything on his own. He opposes your faith in Christ and does everything he can to hinder you and hurt you. He even perverts and abuses God's beautiful creation.

Satan is not equal to God, and he is certainly not omnipotent. He has one purpose:

> *The thief does not come except to steal, and to kill, and to destroy.*
>
> *—John 10:10a*

Satan wants to kill the plan of God and destroy the people of God. He doesn't do anything constructive! Satan is pure evil, and he hates you. You must learn to recognize his plan and his activities before he can barge his way into your mind with conflicting thoughts that solidify into the strongholds he loves so much. If you are not sure what is going on, get some help. Even if you are sure, help is not a bad idea! Remember Moses? Even he needed the help of Aaron and Hur to achieve the victory God intended.

Your Enemy Is Persistent

Let me be clear. Though the enemy does have some favorite strongholds that he tries to build into the lives of Christians, he ultimately doesn't care what strongholds you have, as long as they come between you and God and His love for you.

For example, Satan may not be able to build up a stronghold in my preaching, but he could try to build up a stronghold in my relationship with my wife that affects my preaching. The enemy knows there are multiple ways to achieve his goal. Often, he will attack the people closest to you if he can't affect you directly.

His persistence is something like a loose thread hanging from the hem on your clothing. You pull on it, thinking it will quickly break and disappear, but in seconds, your entire hem has unraveled and you're looking for a safety pin. The enemy is subtle. If you aren't wary, it won't be long before he completely unravels everything around you. But don't be dismayed! As you learn to recognize strongholds, the Lord will empower you to tear them down.

WORKBOOK

Chapter One Questions

Question: In your own words, define *stronghold*. What are the dangers of over- or under-spiritualizing strongholds?

_____

_____

_____

_____

_____

_____

_____

_____

_____

_____

Question: How does Satan use strongholds against believers? Think of an example of this from your own life, either past or present. What can you learn from that experience?

_____

_____

_____

_____

_____

_____

_____

_____

_____

_____

_____

Action: Using this chapter as a starting point, make a list of as many common strongholds as you can think of, particularly those often found among believers. You will use this list in the next chapter.

_____

_____

_____

_____

_____

_____

_____

_____

_____

_____

_____

_____

Chapter One Notes

CHAPTER TWO

Recognizing Strongholds

Have you ever seen a place where people dump their trash illegally? It starts off as an empty lot. Eventually someone realizes it's an empty lot and drops off an unwanted item. Over time, more people recognize this as a dumping ground and begin leaving things they don't want—broken appliances, old furniture, beat-up toys. Unless they're the ones dumping their stuff there, most people don't even notice that the empty lot has become a dumping ground until the pile has grown unreasonably high.

Once you recognize that Satan intends to produce strongholds in your life, you must learn to recognize his devices—how he does it.

The enemy is a master dumper, and his device is to slowly dump garbage into your life until he creates a stronghold. Put a little here, put a little there—most times, you don't even realize it's happening.

I don't have a lot of repair skills, but I do take a little

pride in my front yard. In my opinion, it's the prettiest yard in the neighborhood. I fertilize, water, mow—you name it. But I've noticed there's a patch of weeds I can't seem to get rid of. I didn't realize that these weeds were putting down their roots in time to put down weed killer, so now I must let them grow and work around them. If I try to pull them out, I might pull out the good grass along with them.

In the same way, the enemy tries to mix weeds in with the good growth in our lives. He understands that if you realize who he is but don't recognize in time what he's doing, you won't always be able to pull out what he's done in your life right away. Sometimes, you'll have to let it grow until you can get it out without damaging something else. So before anything else unwanted takes root in your life, let's talk about how to recognize strongholds.

A Conviction or a Stronghold?

A conviction is a clear principle based on Scripture. A stronghold is a belief or thought pattern that you are unwilling or unable to submit to God. A conviction is planted by God, a stronghold by Satan. Often, we struggle with something in between the two: a proclivity—a particular slant on something that is based on personal experience.

Let me give you a prime example. When our children became old enough to want to date, my wife, Millicent, and I realized it would only be a matter of time before they might want to have special friends. Now, the Bible does not address the subject of dating. It doesn't say you can't date, and I know that if I'm going to have grandchildren at some point, my children are going to have to date and get married.

The Bible also doesn't say how people should go about dating, and Millicent and I had different ideas about what would be appropriate. My wife was a little more rigid in her outlook on the matter because she grew up in a household with stricter rules surrounding dating. I, on the other hand, wanted to be involved in matters of communication. In my own dating days, I made a point of introducing myself to the father of the girl I was dating. As I told my daughter, "If you want to talk with someone but he can't come and talk to me, he better not be talking to you." After a lot of discussion, we decided that our children should be sixteen or seventeen before they started dating, which gave them some time to develop good judgment.

I had certain convictions about my children dating. If they dated someone, their date needed to follow our rules. If I told my children they could not date, that would have been unbiblical—a stronghold based on fear.

The Bible has principles that guide us, even if the exact circumstance we face isn't in the Bible. A conviction will never violate His Word. But a stronghold is a mindset or pattern of thinking you have embraced *even though you can't find any support for it in God's Word*. It is especially telling if God tells you to change it and you refuse.

I have another example. People often ask me whether they can smoke cigarettes. That's another topic the Bible does not address. If you're looking for, "Thou shalt not smoke," you won't find it in God's Word. But the Bible does tell us this:

Do you not know that your bodies are temples of the Holy Spirit, who is in you, whom you have received from God? You are not your own; you were bought at a price. Therefore honor God with your bodies.
—1 Corinthians 6:19–20 (NIV)

You may have a legal right to smoke, but as a believer—first and foremost—you belong to the Lord. If smoking is a habit that has mastered you and damages your body, it is wrong. You should also consider how your actions will affect other believers.

Do not destroy the work of God for the sake of food. All food is clean, but it is wrong for a person to eat anything that causes someone else to stumble.
—Romans 14:20 (NIV)

If smoking is going to cause someone else to stumble, you shouldn't do it. If smoking is going to cause someone to misunderstand that God is a deliverer, you shouldn't do it.

I have shared these biblical principles with many people who have asked whether they're free to smoke, and many of them just shrug it off. Since the Bible does not explicitly tell them they can't smoke, they have convinced themselves they're free to do so, no matter what the rest of His Word says. That's not a conviction—that's a stronghold. And because it's taken root in their mind and addicted their bodies, they continue.

Strongholds Can Deceive Anyone

May God himself, the God of peace, sanctify you through and through. May your whole spirit, soul and body be kept blameless at the coming of our Lord Jesus Christ. The one who calls you is faithful, and he will do it.
—*1 Thessalonians 5:23–24 (NIV)*

Therefore let him who thinks he stands take heed lest he fall.
—*1 Corinthians 10:12*

People tend to believe that strongholds only affect unsaved sinners. That is not true, though they may be especially vulnerable. Remember the empty lot that became a dumping ground? The mind of an unsaved person is a natural dumping ground because it is not focused on God or His Word. But when you accept Jesus Christ as your Lord and Savior and the process of sanctification begins, the garbage in your mind needs to go!

If you are a new believer, you shouldn't be surprised to find that the Devil has been at work in your mind. After all, he has had little resistance to his lies up to now. You can be sure that the Lord wants to free you from the prison that Satan has built to torment you. But when old strongholds are torn down, you can bet that new ones are waiting in the wings! The Devil will not give up his attack on your mind easily.

The same can be said if you have been a Christian for many years. Always make sure you are not allowing any action or thought to become more important than following Jesus. Strongholds can be an effective weapon against you. As said before, you must be prepared to fight God's way—in the power of the Holy Spirit.

WORKBOOK

Chapter Two Questions

Question: Have you ever confused a stronghold for a conviction? What is the difference? Give an example from your own life.

_____

_____

_____

_____

_____

_____

_____

_____

_____

_____

_____

_____

Question: How should a believer approach topics that are not specifically addressed in Scripture? How can you be sure you are developing a scriptural conviction as opposed to a stronghold? Where and how does the idea of a "proclivity" fit in?

_____

_____

_____

_____

_____

_____

_____

_____

_____

_____

_____

Action: Using your list from the last chapter and the guidelines in this chapter, ask the Lord to reveal strongholds in your own life. Write down a second, personal list. Prayerfully reflect on how, specifically, to begin breaking down each of these strongholds.

_____

_____

_____

_____

_____

_____

_____

_____

_____

_____

_____

_____

Chapter Two Notes

CHAPTER THREE

Preventing Strongholds

Before we were saved, some of us were straight-up fighters. We weren't about to let anybody walk all over us.

Take that fleshly desire for a fight and ask God to use it for His purposes. Make Satan sorry he ever decided to mess with you!

But how exactly do you prevent the enemy from building up strongholds in your mind? Read the following passages from 2 Corinthians carefully for Paul's answer.

> *Now I, Paul, myself am pleading with you by the meekness and gentleness of Christ—who in presence am lowly among you, but being absent am bold toward you. But I beg you that when I am present I may not be bold with that confidence by which I intend to be bold against some, who think of us as if we walked according to the flesh.*
> **—2 Corinthians 10:1–2**

The context of this passage is that the Corinthian

believers were accusing Paul of being more forceful in his letters to them than he was when he visited them in person. Essentially, they were calling him a coward and saying that he didn't have the guts to correct their doctrine face to face.

For though we walk in the flesh, we do not war according to the flesh. For the weapons of our warfare are not carnal but mighty in God for pulling down strongholds, casting down arguments and every high thing that exalts itself against the knowledge of God, bringing every thought into captivity to the obedience of Christ, and being ready to punish all disobedience when your obedience is fulfilled.

Do you look at things according to the outward appearance? If anyone is convinced in himself that he is Christ's, let him again consider this in himself, that just as he is Christ's, even so we are Christ's. For even if I should boast somewhat more about our authority, which the Lord gave us for edification and not for your destruction, I shall not be ashamed—lest I seem to terrify you by letters. "For his letters," they say, "are weighty and powerful, but his bodily presence is weak, and his speech contemptible." Let such a person consider this, that what we are in word by letters when we are absent, such we will also be in deed when we are present.
—2 Corinthians 10:3–11

Paul responded by reaffirming his calling as an apostle and his authority over the church in Corinth and refuting the false teachers that were trying to take over the Corinthian church. He made it clear to the Corinthian believers that he not only had the authority to correct them and debunk false doctrine but that, if necessary, he would back it up in person. His meekness when he was with them was for their benefit—he could certainly be much bolder if he wanted to be, and he would have no problem doing that if it would keep the Corinthians from believing lies.

For we dare not class ourselves or compare ourselves with those who commend themselves. But they, measuring themselves by themselves, and comparing themselves among themselves, are not wise. We, however, will not boast beyond measure, but within the limits of the sphere which God appointed us—a sphere which especially includes you. For we are not overextending ourselves (as though our authority did not extend to you), for it was to you that we came with the gospel of Christ; not boasting of things beyond measure, that is, in other men's labors, but having hope, that as your faith is increased, we shall be greatly enlarged by you in our sphere, to preach the gospel in the regions beyond you, and not to boast in another man's sphere of accomplishment.

But "he who glories, let him glory in the LORD.*" For not he who commends himself is approved, but whom the Lord commends.*
—2 Corinthians 10:12–18

Paul had reason to be concerned. The lies that the false teachers were spreading to the Corinthians were the enemy's building blocks. If you accept lies, you will not be able to recognize the truth, and accepting lies opens the door for the enemy to build up strongholds.

Paul warned the Corinthians not to misinterpret his meekness as cowardice, and sometimes we also need to remind the enemy we aren't pushovers who'll let him do whatever he wants.

We can prevent strongholds from taking root by filling our minds with the truth of Scripture instead of the lies of the enemy. But what do we do about those strongholds that are already anchored in place? Paul said, "For the weapons of our warfare are not carnal but mighty in God for pulling down strongholds" (2 Corinthians 10:4).

No soldier is sent into combat without first learning how to shoot. And it would clearly be insane for anyone to head into battle with a stick when the enemy is sporting Uzis! Yet how often Christians think they can prevail in spiritual battles with only good intentions. You need to study, to learn, and to strategize to achieve victory. In the next chapter, I will help you devise a battle plan by revealing your weapons and how to use them effectively.

WORKBOOK

Chapter Three Questions

Question: How can you learn to recognize and refute lies before they are ever able to become Satan's "building blocks" to construct a stronghold in your life?

_____

_____

_____

_____

_____

_____

_____

_____

_____

_____

Question: What activates your inner "fight mode"? How can you let God channel this energy toward fighting your true enemy?

_____

_____

_____

_____

_____

_____

_____

_____

_____

_____

_____

Action: *We can prevent strongholds from taking root by filling our minds with the truth of Scripture instead of the lies of the enemy.* What are some ways you can fill your mind with the truth of Scripture? Specifically, what can you look at, or listen to, that will fill your mind with truth? Choose one way and practice it this week.

Chapter Three Notes

_____

_____

_____

_____

_____

_____

_____

_____

_____

_____

_____

_____

_____

_____

_____

_____

_____

_____

_____

_____

_____

_____

CHAPTER FOUR

Know Your Weapons

For though we walk in the flesh, we do not war according to the flesh. For the weapons of our warfare are not carnal but mighty in God for pulling down strongholds, casting down arguments and every high thing that exalts itself against the knowledge of God, bringing every thought into captivity to the obedience of Christ, and being ready to punish all disobedience when your obedience is fulfilled.
—2 Corinthians 10:3-6

The word used for warfare in this passage is the Greek word *strateia*, which refers to an expedition or a military campaign.[2] This definition gives the implication of a long-term battle, not just a skirmish. The tools that help you win the war will never be found in your flesh.

This is why it's so crucial to ask God to renew your mind and your attitude to conform to His Word (Romans 12:2). Paul understood that if you get your mind right, you can mind God right.

If you are trying to operate in the flesh in spiritual warfare, you are eventually going to come up against a demon who will knock you out. Don't even think about fighting that way. You are not fighting a fleshly enemy, so fleshly weapons are a joke to him.

I remember an episode of the TV show *My Wife and Kids* in which Daman Wayans was dealing with Junior, who was his problem child.[3] Daman and Junior were boxing, and Daman boasted that he was going to 'Floyd Mayweather' Junior. Junior caught Daman by surprise and punched him so hard, he folded up and went to sleep. From that day forward, Junior bragged about how he had knocked out his father. You, too, could be the object of a demon's demeaning boast.

> Whoever sows to please their flesh, from the flesh will reap destruction; whoever sows to please the Spirit, from the Spirit will reap eternal life.
> **—Galatians 6:8** *(NIV)*

Let me stress again—your weapons are not carnal, they are spiritual. They are mighty in God when they are used for His purposes. In this case, His purpose is to pull down strongholds. Unfortunately, even spiritual gifts can be abused. If you focus on the gift instead of the Giver, you are in danger of pursuing your own ends instead of God's. A gift used for something other than what God intended will soon prove useless. If you have ever tried to use a screwdriver as a hammer, you get the picture. I have seen many gifted people and preachers abuse their position to coerce and control others.

Unrestricted power also becomes unproductive. For example, you can have the fastest car in the world, but if you speed and drive recklessly, you may lose the privilege of driving that car. If you continue to speed, you may even lose the car—or worse.

The Lord distributes His gifts to many individuals in the body so that no one has to be a superstar problem-solver (Romans 12:3–8). God didn't save you to run amuck or to take on burdens beyond your ability. He saved you to live in an orderly body amid a chaotic world.

Understanding Your Weapons

Paul makes it clear that you need to learn how to use your weapons. They exist to pull down those feelings and thoughts that make you act foolishly. You must get over yourself, get out of yourself, and let God into you. Otherwise, you and the Devil are just going to make a mess of your life, and you will never fulfill God's purpose.

These weapons are designed for "pulling down" strongholds (2 Corinthians 10:4). Picture prayer as a wrecking ball. It batters in both directions as it swings, and you're never sure what direction it will come from next. That is a lot of power. Demons can't just duck and think they are out of range.

The sword of the Spirit, which is the Word of God, that's mentioned in Ephesians 6:17 is described more fully in Hebrews 4:12:

> *For the word of God is living and powerful, and sharper than any two-edged sword, piercing even to the division of soul and spirit, and of joints and marrow, and is a discerner of the thoughts and intents of the heart.*

Paul needed the Corinthians to understand the power of Scripture against the enemy. He is referring here to specific passages that the Spirit brings to your mind when you need them.

When Paul compared these to a two-edged sword, people of his day knew exactly what he meant. A two-edged steel sword hung at the side of every Roman soldier, inspiring fear in the conquered populaces. Some say this sword—called a gladius—was one of the major reasons Roman soldiers were so successful in warfare. They used the gladius primarily for stabbing, so it had a lethal, v-shaped tip. This sword could also slash in either direction, as both edges were sharpened and deadly. Its relatively short length made it especially easy to maneuver. When paired with a shield, the gladius made a Roman soldier a highly effective warrior.[4]

Imagine that sword in hand when you come at your enemy in the heat of battle! Use Scripture to prayerfully resist the Devil and he will flee from you (James 4:7).

Battle Gear

Your weapons, however, will not be as effective if you don't wear your armor. The weapons are offensive—for the attack. The armor is defensive—for your protection. You combat a spiritual enemy. The armor of God enables you to withstand the wiles, the methods, the schemes of the Devil. You can't expect one so evil to just sit still and let you bash him.

Finally, my brethren, be strong in the Lord and in the power of His might. Put on the whole armor of God, that you may be able to stand against the wiles of the devil. For we do not wrestle against flesh and blood, but against principalities, against powers, against the rulers of the darkness of this age, against spiritual hosts of wickedness in the heavenly places. Therefore take up the whole armor of God, that you may be able to withstand in the evil day, and having done all, to stand.

Stand therefore, having girded your waist with truth, having put on the breastplate of righteousness, and having shod your feet with the preparation of the gospel of peace; above all, taking the shield of faith with which you will be able to quench all the fiery darts of the wicked one. And take the helmet of salvation, and the sword of the Spirit, which is the word of God...

—Ephesians 6:10–17

Wear your armor, and lunge. You have everything you need in your spiritual arsenal to inflict serious damage to your ruthless enemy.

Chapter Four Questions

Question: Describe a time when you tried to fight a spiritual battle in fleshly strength. What was the result? What can you learn from that experience for future spiritual battles?

_____

_____

_____

_____

_____

_____

_____

_____

_____

_____

Question: What are the primary weapons of a believer? How can you train yourself to use them so that you are ready when the battle comes?

_____

_____

_____

_____

_____

_____

_____

_____

_____

_____

Action: Do an in-depth study on each piece of spiritual armor described in Ephesians 6. What was its physical purpose for a soldier, and how does that relate to its spiritual purpose for a believer?

Chapter Four Notes

CHAPTER FIVE

Pulling Down Strongholds

Everyone is susceptible to strongholds, but God has commanded us to pull them down. He knows that if we are to move forward, strongholds must be destroyed. They stunt us spiritually and keep us from growing.

So, when you know that you are dealing with a stronghold, you need to make sure you have your wrecking ball (prayer) and sword (the Bible) ready to tear it down.

First, you need to refuse to allow your imagination to dwell on unproductive thoughts. The enemy knows that if he can get certain thoughts to run wild in your mind, he can paralyze your movements. If he can get you to hate church and hate God's people, he can keep you isolated from those you most need to be around. God enables us to keep our thoughts from running wild and settling into the unhealthy patterns that produce strongholds.

Second Corinthians 10:5 tells us that our weapons are effective at "casting down imaginations, and every high thing that exalteth itself against the knowledge of God, and bringing into captivity every thought to the obedience of Christ" (KJV).

God is not against your thinking. He just doesn't want your thinking to be counterproductive. You need to avoid using your imagination for things that work against you— worrying about the what-if's, or how-to's that can consume you completely. He tells you to cast down unproductive thoughts, imaginations, and speculations.

People often tell me that they don't need to go to church, and they don't need the Lord. That is foolish, unproductive speculation. This particular stronghold is within the church as well as outside of it. Yes, you read that right. Even in the church, there are people who believe they can live productive lives without the Lord and encourage others in this delusion.

Remember, Paul addressed his teaching on spiritual warfare to the Corinthian church. He is talking to religious people, not unbelievers. God graciously gives these people time to come to repentance, but in the meantime, the battle against these ideas must be waged continuously.

Another unproductive speculation is the desire for new spiritual experiences. Everyone wants to feel or do something new. As a preacher, I'm essentially only preaching one message:

- God made man.

- Man sinned.

- God sent Jesus.

- Jesus died for man to live.

- Jesus went back to heaven for the Holy Spirit to come live within man.

- And Jesus will come again.

That's pretty much it.

But you can reject the simplicity and clarity of the gospel if you pursue vain speculation about spiritual phenomena. You become so focused on chasing new experiences that you lose your appreciation of all that God has already done for you. And that's the enemy's goal. He doesn't want you to desire the God who has given you new life, the God whose mercy is new every morning (Lamentations 3:23)—the God who knew you in your mother's womb (Psalm 139:13), who shelters you in the shadow of His wings (Psalm 91:4), who sent His Son to die for you (John 3:16). In short, Satan does not want you to love Jesus and live for Him.

He wants you to feel discontent and unsatisfied, even if you were in the Garden of Eden. Remember Adam and Eve (Genesis 3)? They were living in fellowship with God until Satan presented them with a lie and stirred discontent in their hearts.

When you realize that your mind can be full of self-defeating nonsense, the natural response is to want to be rid of it. You cry for the Spirit's help, and He understands. He has already paved the way for you to be free.

Take Every Thought Captive

Perhaps you have such undisciplined thoughts that you

have allowed your mind to become a playground for fool-
ishness, and you are not equipped to build something of
structure and status. God knows that if He gets your mind,
He will ultimately get your soul. But if He cannot get your
mind, it is that much harder for Him to get your soul.

You cannot afford to let your thoughts run wild. Paul
said you should use your God-given weapons:

> ...casting down arguments and every high thing that exalts
> itself against the knowledge of God, bringing every
> thought into captivity to the obedience of Christ...
> —2 Corinthians 10:5

You must take every thought captive—pay attention to
it, examine it—even if it seems like a good thought.
Sometimes the enemy will give you a good thought to mo-
tivate you to do the wrong thing. He is not a gentleman.
He doesn't play fair.

A good example is when David decided to bring the
ark of the covenant up to Jerusalem. It was a good idea,
but he went about it the wrong way:

> Again David gathered all the choice men of Israel, thirty
> thousand. And David arose and went with all the people
> who were with him from Baale Judah to bring up from
> there the ark of God, whose name is called by the Name,
> the LORD of Hosts, who dwells between the cherubim. So
> they set the ark of God on a new cart, and brought it out of
> the house of Abinadab, which was on the hill; and Uzzah
> and Ahio, the sons of Abinadab, drove the new cart. And
> they brought it out of the house of Abinadab, which was on
> the hill, accompanying the ark of God; and Ahio went be-
> fore the ark. Then David and all the house of Israel played

music before the LORD on all kinds of instruments of fir
wood, on harps, on stringed instruments, on tambourines,
on sistrums, and on cymbals.

And when they came to Nachon's threshing floor, Uzzah
put out his hand to the ark of God and took hold of it, for
the oxen stumbled. Then the anger of the LORD was aroused
against Uzzah, and God struck him there for his error; and
he died there by the ark of God. And David became angry
because of the LORD's outbreak against Uzzah; and he
called the name of the place Perez Uzzah to this day.
—2 Samuel 6:1-8

Since there weren't any Levites with David to carry the
ark, David decided to put it on a cart. Bad idea. God had
said that only the Levites should carry the ark. If David
had taken that thought captive and evaluated it, he would
have realized the idea was not in alignment with God's
prescribed way. He would have concluded that he needed
to move the ark the way God said it should be moved. But
David did not take that thought captive. As a result, Uzzah, who is not a Levite, touched the ark and died.

The enemy knows that if you don't restrain your
thoughts, you may overlook something very important to
the Lord. Satan is very good at planting seemingly good
ideas to make you do something wrong.

Take humanity's critical failure in the Garden of Eden
(Genesis 3). The serpent—Satan—told Eve that the fruit
of that tree was good to eat because it would make her
wise (Genesis 3:4–5). This was a half-truth that stirred
Eve's curiosity. If Eve had taken that thought captive, she
would have remembered that God had warned Adam and
her not to eat that fruit or they would die. Adam did not
take the thought captive either, and he failed both Eve and

God by his complicity. All creation became captive to sin by Adam and Eve's lack of vigilance and obedience.

Every thought must be taken captive to God and what is in His Word, the Bible. If He does not say that it is right, it is not right. When the Devil argues this point, take the thought captive. Look it up in Scripture. Ask the Holy Spirit for discernment. Don't take Satan's word for it. He lies. Tear down the lies intended to create a stronghold before Satan has the time to fortify that stronghold in your life.

WORKBOOK

Chapter Five Questions

Question: What are some areas in which you allow your thoughts and imagination to run wild? How has this led, or could it lead, to strongholds in these areas?

_____

_____

_____

_____

_____

_____

_____

_____

_____

_____

_____

_____

Question: Have you ever had a good idea that you pursued in an unbiblical way? How could things have turned out differently if you had taken your thoughts captive first?

_____

_____

_____

_____

_____

_____

_____

_____

_____

_____

_____

Action: Practice "thinking about what you're thinking about." For a full day, jot down a list of everything you think about. In what areas is your mind most vulnerable to Satan's attacks?

Chapter Five Notes

_____

_____

_____

_____

_____

_____

_____

_____

_____

_____

_____

_____

_____

_____

_____

_____

_____

_____

_____

_____

_____

_____

Part Two: Walls

CHAPTER SIX

How Walls Are Formed

The name of the LORD is a strong tower; the righteous run to it and are safe.

—Proverbs 18:10

Some walls serve a good purpose, confining what should stay in and restricting what should stay out. These are God's walls, and they need to stay in place.

For example, when you live within the confines of righteousness and God's dominion—you are safe. Once you wander out, you are subject to the wiles of the enemy and his minions.

But the enemy uses walls of a different kind, walls that you build in your mind to protect yourself from past hurts or a hostile environment. Note the very next verse in Proverbs 18:

The rich man's wealth is his strong city, and like a high wall in his own esteem.

—Proverbs 18:11

The irony of riches and self-esteem is that they are fragile and can be easily breached and destroyed. They are walls built in our own image and with our own resources. They do not possess the protection that following God's way provides for us. When we build walls with our own strength and resources, they isolate us from God and His people.

These walls keep the bad things in and the good things out and make the perfect opportunity for Satan to take advantage of us. These walls are not able to be penetrated or skirted. *They must come down.* Thankfully, God gives us the ability and tools to tear down walls, just as He does with strongholds.

If you can keep your mind in Jesus and on Jesus, you will be able to recognize foolish talk when you hear it. You will recognize when the enemy is speaking lies to you and trying to dredge up fear and insecurity.

But if you are not secure in the safety of abiding in Christ, you may be tempted to erect isolating walls to "protect" yourself. At that point, Satan has what he needs to build a wall between you and God.

Remember, a stronghold is a state of mind where you are so thoroughly convinced of a thought pattern that you cannot or will not submit it to the will of God. You believe the stronghold is reality, and you cannot convince yourself that God has anything better for you. A stronghold left intact can lead to a wall that cuts you off from the provisions of God.

For instance, you might think you'll never be a good leader. You might think you can never be a good parent or a good spouse. These strongholds create walls in your mind. The walls become so fortified that you start living your life in a way that accommodates those thoughts and prevents you from having access to the promises of God.

This is not God's plan for you.

No Compromise

Let's look at one of the best-known walls in the Bible—the wall of Jericho. This was a wall that had to come down if Israel was to reach God's plan for them.

> *Now Jericho was securely shut up because of the children of Israel; none went out, and none came in.*
> **—Joshua 6:1**

The people of Jericho had heard of the Israelites crossing the Jordan on dry land. They could probably see the masses of people coming across the desert from the dust they raised. Jericho was afraid, so the inhabitants locked up the city behind its walls. The city of Jericho wasn't letting anyone out, and it wasn't letting anyone in.

The problem was that Jericho was in the promised land, the land that God had promised to the Israelites. If Jericho was allowed to stand, the Israelites would never be able to claim what was rightfully theirs. This was the first test of their resolve. With God's help and direction, the walls fell

(Joshua 6:20–21).

The enemy knows that the moment you start trying to get your mind right, God will bring you into the life He has promised you. The last thing Satan wants is the Word of God filling your mind and heart. He will try to make a deal with you to keep you from tearing down walls. He'll try to convince you that the walls aren't really a threat—they're just standing there. If you permit these walls to stay, Satan will eventually use them to move in. Those walls may not seem dangerous today, but Satan wants to control you and neutralize your witness. Once you have the Word of God coming in, those walls are coming down.

The enemy doesn't want that. He wants ungodly thoughts to stay behind the walls, to remain locked up tight in your inner Jericho. He knows that if those thoughts leave the safety of those walls, you can take them captive to the Word of God, and you can change them (2 Corinthians 10:5). Once that happens, it's over for him.

Perhaps you still wonder why you would build walls when they seem so counterproductive. How are they used? How do you avoid them? Read on to the next chapter and see what God's Word tells us.

WORKBOOK

Chapter Six Questions

Question: What are some significant past hurts or difficulties you have faced? How might these create specific temptations to "build a wall" to protect yourself?

_____

_____

_____

_____

_____

_____

_____

_____

_____

_____

_____

Question: Why is right thinking such a threat to Satan? What steps can you take to develop right thinking in your internal life?

_____

_____

_____

_____

_____

_____

_____

_____

_____

_____

_____

Action: Read Joshua chapters 2–7. What were some specific "walls" of ungodly thinking that the Israelites had to work through on their end—both prior to and after the battle—before God's power could give them victory?

Chapter Six Notes

_____

_____

_____

_____

_____

_____

_____

_____

_____

_____

_____

_____

_____

_____

_____

_____

_____

_____

_____

_____

_____

_____

CHAPTER SEVEN

The Worldly Face of Walls

Walls have certain charms. They give you a sense of possession and permanence. Walls seem strong and make you think you need them, like you can't survive without them. You feel that being without them is like being naked in public.

People can hook you, saying that you need to act a certain way so that others won't take advantage of you or to be successful in life. They urge you to follow the crowd for the sake of inclusion. What they often promote is sin. But groupthink, "a pattern of thought characterized by self-deception, forced manufacture of consent, and conformity to group values and ethics," has a certain attraction.[5] It can feel like a supportive family. So, you put up walls to shut out the truth about what gives you strength. But what does the Bible say?

...He who is in you is greater than he who is in the world.
—1 John 4:4

My help comes from the LORD, who made heaven and earth.
—Psalm 121:2

No weapon formed against you shall prosper...
—Isaiah 54:17

You don't need to lower your standards to be popular or significant. You don't have to engage in toxic, sinful behavior to survive in this world. Don't allow the enemy to trick you into thinking you need these kinds of walls to bring you happiness and success.

Walls Block the Son

The enemy knows that if you put up enough walls, he can keep you away from Scripture and those people that help you see God in your life. You become so used to the walls blocking your perception that you don't really pay attention to them after a while. The sense of isolation can be overwhelming. Other people say God is moving, but you can't see Him or make any sense of what He is doing. You think it would be easier if you just stopped trying. If you don't seek God, you won't spend time building your relationship with Him. You will remain walled up like the city of Jericho.

The presence of God is everything. Without it, you become as desolate as an abandoned city.

...in Your presence is fullness of joy; at Your right hand are pleasures forevermore.
—Psalm 16:11b

Before Joshua could attack Jericho and start dealing with those walls, he needed to be assured of the fact that God was on his side. Joshua came back to the power and the presence of the Lord (Joshua 5:13–15). No one is going to drag you back into the presence of God. Like Joshua, you need to take those steps on your own two feet and recognize the walls for what they are— so you can bring them down.

Walls of Doubt

Doubt is one of the enemy's favorite tools because doubt can be as strong as faith. Faith honors God, but doubt hinders His work. Nothing can stop God, but the Bible tells us that Jesus did not do many miracles in his hometown of Nazareth because the people doubted Him.

> When He had come to His own country, He taught them in their synagogue, so that they were astonished and said, "Where did this Man get this wisdom and these mighty works? Is this not the carpenter's son? Is not His mother called Mary? And His brothers James, Joses, Simon, and Judas? And His sisters, are they not all with us? Where then did this Man get all these things?" So they were offended at Him.
>
> But Jesus said to them, "A prophet is not without honor except in his own country and in his own house." Now He did not do many mighty works there because of their unbelief.
> **—Matthew 13:54–58**

Doubt makes you believe that things can never be better than they are, that there's no room for improvement, no room for miracles. A life lived doubting is a life bereft of God's intervention. The enemy doesn't want you to believe that God can help you to change, and so he keeps reinforcing that wall of doubt with his half-truths and lies.

Choose the Right Cause

I came that they may have life, and have it abundantly.
—John 10:10b (NASB)

Every now and then, you need to take inventory of your life and check whether the walls in your mind are good walls that support God's purposes or bad walls protecting Satan's strongholds. If they're not for God, it's time to issue some heavenly eviction notices. You don't need anything in your mind, anything in your heart, anything in your life that's not for God.

God is never angry at us for asking questions. But once you ask a question and God gives you an answer, you need to do what He says. Even if you don't ask a question but God lets you know that something is required of you, you need to do what He says. Not asking does not excuse disobedience when the Lord makes Himself clear.

No matter what you think or how you allow the enemy to fool you, you need to make choices in your life. If you choose not to choose God, that is a choice in and of itself—and it's the wrong choice. Even not choosing is in fact a choice. Don't leave it in the enemy's court. Choose to tear down all destructive walls, *all* that keep you from the abundant life Jesus won for you.

WORKBOOK

Chapter Seven Questions

Question: What are some areas in your life where you are doubting God? What type of situations make you most vulnerable to doubt? How does doubt put a wall between you and God?

_____

_____

_____

_____

_____

_____

_____

_____

_____

_____

Question: Describe a time when you asked God a question but then didn't want to live within His answer. Did you ultimately choose obedience or disobedience? What happened as a result?

_____

_____

_____

_____

_____

_____

_____

_____

_____

_____

_____

Action: _Every now and then, you need to take inventory of your life and check whether the walls in your mind are good walls that support God's purposes or bad walls protecting Satan's strongholds._ Set aside a time to journal about this. Ask God to reveal good walls of righteousness that you need to shore up as well as ungodly walls of self-preservation and doubt that you need to tear down.

Chapter Seven Notes

_____

_____

_____

_____

_____

_____

_____

_____

_____

_____

_____

_____

_____

_____

_____

_____

_____

_____

_____

_____

_____

_____

CHAPTER EIGHT

Delusions of Grandeur

Walls can have a significant impact on your relationship with God. Since they block you from seeing God, you might forget your position relative to Him. When that happens, you yourself become the center of your world, not God. Your needs, your desires, your pleasures become the focus of your thoughts and prayers.

You need to spend time in His presence to realize who He is and who you are. He is exalted. He is God—there's no one higher. Stop exalting yourself and get off the throne. Look to the hills from whence your help comes, knowing that your help comes from the Lord (Psalm 121:1–2).

Humble Yourself

Digress with me a moment. Your favorite sports team may have skilled and qualified players, but when they come up against a team that's more skilled, they must step up their game. Say your team has gotten through the playoffs, but now they're in the finals. They need to focus now on beating their competition. You don't get the trophy for doing well in the playoffs. You only get the trophy if you win the final game.

So now back to you. You may have already beaten inferior competition, tearing down walls that were smaller or weaker, but every now and then, you will encounter one that's particularly stubborn and requires major demolition. If you've become high-minded, thinking of yourself more highly than you should, it doesn't matter what tactics you use. You'll still lose the battle if you rely only on yourself and your own resources.

God is greater than we are, and that's something we're prone to forget. We need to humble ourselves before Him and acknowledge that the walls that are bigger than us are not bigger than He is.

The Holiness of God

Our culture has made God common. Christmas is now Xmas, and in school, Christmas break is now labeled "winter break." Jesus' name is an everyday curse word. God's creation of the universe is a subject for debate. Atheists—on the rise all over the world—postulate that they have the right to decide whether God even exists. We have become more concerned about not hurting others' feelings than honoring God. How utterly absurd.

God is not common; He is holy. Uzzah touched the ark and died because God is holy (2 Samuel 6:6–8). When Isaiah encountered the Lord, he was so overwhelmed by

God's holiness that he despaired over his own sinfulness.

In the year that King Uzziah died, I saw the Lord sitting on a throne, high and lifted up, and the train of His robe filled the temple. Above it stood seraphim; each one had six wings: with two he covered his face, with two he covered his feet, and with two he flew. And one cried to another and said: "Holy, holy, holy is the LORD of hosts; The whole earth is full of His glory!"

And the posts of the door were shaken by the voice of him who cried out, and the house was filled with smoke. So I said: "Woe is me, for I am undone! Because I am a man of unclean lips, And I dwell in the midst of a people of unclean lips; For my eyes have seen the King, The LORD of hosts."

Then one of the seraphim flew to me, having in his hand a live coal which he had taken with the tongs from the altar. And he touched my mouth with it, and said: "Behold, this has touched your lips; Your iniquity is taken away, And your sin purged."

—Isaiah 6:1–7

When God appeared to Moses in the burning bush, Moses had to take off his sandals, for the holiness of God is such that even the ground where Moses stood was holy.

Now Moses was tending the flock of Jethro his father-in-law, the priest of Midian. And he led the flock to the back of the desert, and came to Horeb, the mountain of God. And the Angel of the LORD appeared to him in a flame of fire from the midst of a bush. So he looked, and behold, the bush was burning with fire, but the bush was not consumed. Then Moses said, "I will now turn aside and see this great sight, why the bush does not burn."

So when the LORD saw that he turned aside to look, God called to him from the midst of the bush and said, "Moses,

Moses!" And he said, "Here I am."

Then He said, "Do not draw near this place. Take your sandals off your feet, for the place where you stand is holy ground." Moreover He said, "I am the God of your father— the God of Abraham, the God of Isaac, and the God of Jacob." And Moses hid his face, for he was afraid to look upon God.

—Exodus 3:1–6

We see similar reactions to God's holiness over and over in the Bible. Daniel fainted (Daniel 10:7–9). Ezekiel fell on his face (Ezekiel 1:28). Fear fell on Zacharias and he was rendered mute for his disbelief (Luke 1:8–22). In the Garden of Gethsemane, Roman soldiers fell to the ground dazed (John 18:6). The guards at Jesus's tomb shook with fear and became like dead men (Matthew 28:4). Paul was knocked off his horse and blinded (Acts 9:3–9). Mind you, these men did not see God face to face, but even the angels who came as God's messengers carried the power and authority of His presence.

Pursue peace with everyone, and the holiness without which no one will see the Lord...

—Hebrews 12:14

No. Our God is not common. He is so holy that even those He summoned by name in Scripture could not stand in His presence. In this hellish world where culture and circumstances may tempt us to forget, we must continually ask God to remind us of His holiness and the need for our own holiness in Christ. If we want to tear down our walls, we must first humble ourselves and recognize the unparalleled holiness of God.

WORKBOOK

Chapter Eight Questions

Question: Consider the things you pray for most regularly. Do your prayers reflect a focus on yourself or on God? What walls in your life might be skewing your view of God?

_____

_____

_____

_____

_____

_____

_____

_____

_____

_____

Question: How do you see God treated as "common" in our culture? In what ways do you yourself fall into this trap?

_____

_____

_____

_____

_____

_____

_____

_____

_____

_____

Action: Make out a list of God's amazing names and attributes found in Scripture. Spend some designated time in prayer and praise, focusing exclusively on who God is, not your own needs or desires.

Chapter Eight Notes

CHAPTER NINE

Pulling Down Walls

How do you pull down walls?

You need to follow God's battle plan. That sounds simple, but God's way of doing things doesn't always make sense to us.

> *"For My thoughts are not your thoughts, nor are your ways My ways," says the LORD. "For as the heavens are higher than the earth, so are My ways higher than your ways, and My thoughts than your thoughts."*
> **—Isaiah 55:8–9**

There may be times when believe you want God to move in your life, but in actuality, you want Him to work according to your plan. However, your own assessment of the situation and how to resolve it may be completely off the track. Instead of telling God what you think about the walls in your mind and heart, ask Him what He thinks and what He wants to do.

When my wife and I have a discussion, she often

reminds me that discussion is a process in which two people exchange ideas. She gets to say something, I get to say something. I'll admit that discussions are not my strong suit. I'm a good talker. I figure that once I've spoken, the discussion should be over. There have been times when I've thought out my plan, presented my plan, and considered that the end of the discussion.

When that happens, Millicent will ask, "Do you need me in this plan?" I say, "Well, didn't we already discuss your part in the plan?" If I'm giving her a part in the plan, she feels she should have a say in what the plan is and what part she's going to play. It doesn't work well when I try to do it for her.

The Lord wants to be invited into your plan, too. That is what prayer is about. He loves discussions.

God's Procedure

Let's look at Joshua before he marched on Jericho again (Joshua 6). After Joshua put God in His rightful position and praised Him, God gave Joshua a procedure. Obvious to any man of war, God's plan was unconventional but utterly successful. It provides a blueprint for dealing with walls in your life and mine.

First, notice that walls require confrontation, not accommodation.

> *And the LORD said to Joshua: "See! I have given Jericho into your hand, its king, and the mighty men of valor."*
> *—Joshua 6:2*

God does not say He's going to give Jericho to Joshua. He doesn't ask Joshua if he wants Jericho. He tells him He *has given* him Jericho. God made it clear to Joshua that the walls around Jericho were not serving His purposes and needed to come down.

And the walls weren't coming down until someone confronted them. God told Joshua exactly what to do about Jericho's walls. Joshua only needed to obey His instructions.

You shall march around the city, all you men of war; you shall go all around the city once. This you shall do six days. And seven priests shall bear seven trumpets of rams' horns before the ark. But the seventh day you shall march around the city seven times, and the priests shall blow the trumpets. It shall come to pass, when they make a long blast with the ram's horn, and when you hear the sound of the trumpet, that all the people shall shout with a great shout; then the wall of the city will fall down flat. And the people shall go up every man straight before him.
—Joshua 6:3–5

Talk to the Lord and to others you trust about walls you think may be locking up your mind. Once you're aware that certain walls or strongholds do exist, ask God for His specific plan of confrontation.

Secondly, if you're going to tear down a wall, you need to go to the wall. It's not going to come to you. Since these walls are in our lives because we've accommodated them, sometimes we're reluctant to confront them. It's important to remember that tearing down a wall doesn't happen all at once. It's a process.

Thirdly, you also need to circle that wall daily in

prayer to determine if any wayward thoughts try to sneak out from behind it. And when they do, you take those thoughts captive to the Word of God. March them over to God as prisoners and let Him tell you what to do with them.

Next, when facing your wall, you need to be obedient to the leading of the Lord. Joshua rallied the people to do what God said:

> Then Joshua the son of Nun called the priests and said to them, "Take up the ark of the covenant, and let seven priests bear seven trumpets of rams' horns before the ark of the LORD." And he said to the people, "Proceed, and march around the city, and let him who is armed advance before the ark of the LORD."
>
> So it was, when Joshua had spoken to the people, that the seven priests bearing the seven trumpets of rams' horns before the LORD advanced and blew the trumpets, and the ark of the covenant of the LORD followed them. The armed men went before the priests who blew the trumpets, and the rear guard came after the ark, while the priests continued blowing the trumpets. Now Joshua had commanded the people, saying, "You shall not shout or make any noise with your voice, nor shall a word proceed out of your mouth, until the day I say to you, 'Shout!' Then you shall shout." So he had the ark of the LORD circle the city, going around it once. Then they came into the camp and lodged in the camp.
>
> **—Joshua 6:6–11**

This procession and the sound of the trumpets made it clear to the enemy that the Lord was fighting the battle, not the Israelites circling the city. Likewise, if you confront your walls and follow God's procedure, the enemy knows he's fighting the Lord and cannot win.

The fifth important aspect of God's blueprint for deal-ing with walls is to trust that He is in control. Even if you feel like you're going in circles and making no progress, God is working on your behalf. The enemy will try to dis-courage you, telling you that there's no way that wall is ever coming down. When that happens, imagine the trum-pets blowing and that God is going to do it His way, even though you can't see how it's possible.

> *The things which are impossible with men are possible with God.*
> **—Luke 18:27**

Finally, praise will bring the ultimate breakthrough. This is demonstrated by the final cry of the Israelites unto the Lord.

> But it came to pass on the seventh day that they rose early, about the dawning of the day, and marched around the city seven times in the same manner. On that day only, they marched around the city seven times. And the seventh time it happened, when the priests blew the trumpets, that Joshua said to the people: "Shout, for the LORD has given you the city!"
> **—Joshua 6:15–16**

This was the only day the Israelites circled the wall seven times. The number seven signifies total dependence on God. The enemy, who had no idea what was about to happen, was probably laughing to himself. Why did they think anything would be any different this day?

During those first six days, the Israelites only had to be silent and blow the trumpets and let God work in their midst. But when it came time for that wall to come down, the Lord commanded them to shout in praise. Sometimes you need to remind the enemy that you're only being silent until God tells you to shout. In fact, your silence should terrify him given what happened at Jericho.

Worth the Effort

Pulling down a wall God's way requires patience and trust. It takes time to circle that wall day after day, but it is worth the effort. You may wonder why you must do it that way, why you must keep dealing with it, but your work will be rewarded.

It reminds me of when my mother made chitterlings. For those of you who have never had this dish, chitterlings are made from the small intestines of a pig. As you can imagine, making them involves some unpleasantness, some stink. But I can tell you, when the chitterlings come together with rice and hot sauce, it is well worth the wait and any unpleasantness that may have been involved in the process. I love those chitterlings!

But the weapons of our warfare are not carnal. The Israelites didn't break down the wall with their own power. They yielded their spirit and let God do what He had promised.

Even the youths shall faint and be weary, and the young men shall utterly fall, but those who wait on the LORD shall

renew their strength; they shall mount up with wings like
eagles, they shall run and not be weary, they shall walk and
not faint.
                                    —Isaiah 40:31–32

I'm sure there was some grumbling among the Israelites during those six days of circling the city. People were
probably asking why they had to keep doing the same
thing, even though the sound of the trumpets didn't seem
to accomplish anything.

But Joshua was a Proverbs 3:5–6 kind of guy: "Trust
in the LORD with all your heart, and lean not on your own
understanding; in all your ways acknowledge Him, and
He shall direct your paths." Joshua trusted in the Lord.
After all, he had been with Moses all the way from Egypt,
watching God work for forty years. And when you trust
God above your own understanding, you can be sure that
He directs your paths—even if you're going around in circles.

And the Bible tells us that that wall did indeed come
down:

So the people shouted when the priests blew the trumpets.
And it happened when the people heard the sound of the
trumpet, and the people shouted with a great shout, that
the wall fell down flat. Then the people went up into the
city, every man straight before him, and they took the city.
                                    —Joshua 6:20

God made it clear to the Israelites that they were not to
take anything out of Jericho (Joshua 6:17–19). If your
walls come down, you don't want to hold on to anything

that God has destroyed. He got you out; don't even think about going back. Remember, walls are built when you accommodate foolish thoughts. The enemy knows that it's okay for him to lose the wall if he can make you hold on to the thoughts that caused it.

Be Still and Know That He Is God

Remember the former things of old, for I am God, and there is no other; I am God, and there is none like Me, declaring the end from the beginning, and from ancient times things that are not yet done, saying, "My counsel shall stand, and I will do all My pleasure..."

—Isaiah 46:9–10

God knows everything. Nothing escapes His notice, and everything about your life is merged into His plan for you. He knew your physical body wasn't going to be the same size from birth to death, so He made allowances for you. He designed you so that your skin could stretch, and your bones were strong enough to carry you. The same is true of your spirit. He sees the end from the beginning and guides your path through His Holy Spirit and His Word.

There's no need to fear. You can trust God. If you do what He commands you to do, He will do His part.

Obedience to God is the only way to the promised land, where you can enjoy your soul's salvation. Walls may create a barrier, but they will be short-lived if you follow God's procedure to bring them down. Trust Him and watch them crumble with a shout of praise.

WORKBOOK

Chapter Nine Questions

Question: How would it change your approach if you believed that God has already given you victory over the strongholds in your life?

_____

_____

_____

_____

_____

_____

_____

_____

_____

_____

Question: Describe a time when obeying God meant doing something that looked crazy from an outside view. What did He teach you through your obedience?

_____

_____

_____

_____

_____

_____

_____

_____

_____

_____

Action: Joshua was able to trust and depend on God, even when He prescribed a "strange" way to victory, because he'd witnessed God's faithfulness and provision already over the past forty years or so. How have you seen God's faithfulness in your own past? What incidents from your own life remind you that you can trust Him for victory in your current struggle?

Chapter Nine Notes

Part Three: Giants

CHAPTER TEN

Giants Are Different

When Joshua and the Israelites confronted Jericho, they had to go to Jericho. Jericho didn't go to them. Walls stay where they are. Likewise, strongholds stay in one place, and you can confront them bit by bit over time.

Giants, however, *follow you*. They get in your face and challenge you when you least expect it—and they refuse to back down. They force you to deal with them.

Goliath is perhaps the most famous giant of history and has become a metaphor for overwhelming situations in life. He was a formidable foe. Scholars believe that he would've been anywhere from seven and a half to nine and half feet tall. He would've been the ancient equivalent of the famous professional wrestler, Andre the Giant.[6]

In this passage, the Philistines and the Israelites were at odds, and the Philistines were trying to take land that rightfully belonged to the Israelites. With Goliath as their champion, the Philistines figured the Israelites had no choice but to give in.

Now the Philistines gathered their armies together to battle, and were gathered at Sochoh, which belongs to Judah; they encamped between Sochoh and Azekah, in Ephes Dammim. And Saul and the men of Israel were gathered together, and they encamped in the Valley of Elah, and drew up in battle array against the Philistines. The Philistines stood on a mountain on one side, and Israel stood on a mountain on the other side, with a valley between them.

And a champion went out from the camp of the Philistines, named Goliath, from Gath, whose height was six cubits and a span. He had a bronze helmet on his head, and he was armed with a coat of mail, and the weight of the coat was five thousand shekels of bronze. And he had bronze armor on his legs and a bronze javelin between his shoulders. Now the staff of his spear was like a weaver's beam, and his iron spearhead weighed six hundred shekels; and a shield-bearer went before him. Then he stood and cried out to the armies of Israel, and said to them, "Why have you come out to line up for battle? Am I not a Philistine, and you the servants of Saul? Choose a man for yourselves, and let him come down to me. If he is able to fight with me and kill me, then we will be your servants. But if I prevail against him and kill him, then you shall be our servants and serve us." And the Philistine said, "I defy the armies of Israel this day; give me a man, that we may fight together."
—1 Samuel 17:1–10

Giants like Goliath overwhelm us and make us think they're undefeatable. You may not have to fight a giant today or tomorrow, but you'll have to fight one someday. And you need to know that they can be overcome through God's strength. You need to believe that giants do fall. Our God is big, our God is strong, and there is nothing He cannot do. You may not feel it in your flesh, but you can know it in the Spirit.

*Behold, I am the LORD, the God of all flesh. Is there anything
too hard for Me?*

—*Jeremiah 32:27*

Today's Giants

The enemy knows your giant, and he will use it against
you. My giant was alcohol. Although I was truly delivered
from it, I had to have a conversation with alcohol and declare my freedom again.

I wasn't going to bars or clubs for liquor. My danger
zone was the 7-Eleven. They sell more than Slurpees
there, you know. As I walked to the coolers to get a soda,
I could hear the Bartles & Jaymes wine coolers calling my
name.

The enemy encouraged me to go over and say hello.
Since I had defeated the giant of alcohol, he argued, there
was no danger in looking. All I did was look and check
out the variety. Since their packaging was green, I rea-
soned, if someone I knew happened to see me, I could
always tell them I had a bottle of Mountain Dew. Before
I knew it, I found myself on the verge of picking up a wine
cooler because my giant was pursuing me and beckoning
me to come and drink. And I almost lost the battle.

I knew that if I was going to fulfill my calling as a believer—lust wasn't a problem, snuff wasn't a problem—
that bottle was absolutely a problem. It couldn't stand. I
needed to defeat my giant.

What about the giant that calls your name—the giant you can't run away from? Your giant might lull you with a destructive high. Your giant may want you to compromise your purity to make extra cash. Perhaps your giant tells you it's okay to spend money needed for groceries on makeup or clothes, instead. Or maybe your giant says you're justified in mistreating your spouse or children because that's how you were raised. The list is long and ugly.

Temptation is powerful, and our culture does more to promote it than fight it. Satan knows that if you're going be the believer you're called to be, you'll have defeat your giant—and he knows you're afraid to fight. But God is not, and He knows that giants do fall.

An Everyday Fight

Remember, "the weapons of our warfare are not carnal but mighty in God for pulling down strongholds" (2 Corinthians 10:4). You cannot fight a giant in your flesh. If you're going to help yourself, you need to get out of yourself.

You are your own worst enemy. If you had enough willpower to stop caving in and letting this giant take what belongs to you, you would've stopped a long time ago. You might lecture yourself every day about why you must stop, but you never act.

For I know that in me (that is, in my flesh) nothing good dwells; for to will is present with me, but how to perform what is good I do not find.

—Romans 7:18

Our bodies are neutral in principle, but if we don't focus on God and feed our minds with Scripture, our natural minds will take our neutral flesh into some ungodly territory. Spiritual warfare is an ongoing part of our lives as believers. God brought the Israelites into the promised land, but He didn't kill all the giants. After Jericho, there was another battle at Ai (Joshua 7). Fighting the enemy is not a one-time thing; it's a crucial part of our Christian walk.

In Acts 16, Paul encountered the giant of divination:

Now it happened, as we went to prayer, that a certain slave girl possessed with a spirit of divination met us, who brought her masters much profit by fortune-telling. This girl followed Paul and us, and cried out, saying, "These men are the servants of the Most High God, who proclaim to us the way of salvation." And this she did for many days.

—Acts 16:16–18a

Paul was vexed by this situation, and he knew he needed to call this spirit out. The people knew that this slave girl worshiped and served a false god, but now she was saying that Paul and Silas were proclaiming the true God. Could that mean her god was true, too? Paul knew that this lying spirit confused many people.

But Paul, greatly annoyed, turned and said to the spirit, "I command you in the name of Jesus Christ to come out of her." And he came out that very hour.

Lot is another example of an individual who was pursued by a giant. Second Peter 2:6–8 tells us that God
turned "the cities of Sodom and Gomorrah into ashes,
condemned them to destruction, making them an example
to those who afterward would live ungodly; and delivered
righteous Lot, who was oppressed by the filthy conduct of
the wicked (for that righteous man, dwelling among them,
tormented his righteous soul from day to day by seeing
and hearing their lawless deeds)."

Lot was so overwhelmed by the giant of ungodliness
that overshadowed the city in which he lived, he couldn't
even begin to confront it. God had to come and rescue Lot
and his family. As you will read in Genesis 19:1–16, Lot
did the best he could in the middle of horrible circumstances:

> Now the two angels came to Sodom in the evening, and Lot
> was sitting in the gate of Sodom. When Lot saw them, he
> rose to meet them, and he bowed himself with his face to-
> ward the ground. And he said, "Here now, my lords, please
> turn in to your servant's house and spend the night, and
> wash your feet; then you may rise early and go on your
> way." And they said, "No, but we will spend the night in the
> open square."
>
> But he insisted strongly; so they turned in to him and en-
> tered his house. Then he made them a feast, and baked
> unleavened bread, and they ate.

Lot offered the strangers hospitality, an act that

underlines his righteous nature. In what follows, there is a sharp contrast between godly Lot and the wicked men of Sodom.

> *Now before they lay down, the men of the city, the men of Sodom, both old and young, all the people from every quarter, surrounded the house. And they called to Lot and said to him, "Where are the men who came to you tonight? Bring them out to us that we may know them carnally."*
>
> *So Lot went out to them through the doorway, shut the door behind him, and said, "Please, my brethren, do not do so wickedly! See now, I have two daughters who have not known a man; please, let me bring them out to you, and you may do to them as you wish; only do nothing to these men, since this is the reason they have come under the shadow of my roof."*

The men of Sodom intended to gang rape the visitors, whom Lot desperately attempted to protect, even going to the extent of offering to bring out his daughters instead of the visitors.

> *And they said, "Stand back!" Then they said, "This one came in to stay here, and he keeps acting as a judge; now we will deal worse with you than with them." So they pressed hard against the man Lot, and came near to break down the door. But the men reached out their hands and pulled Lot into the house with them, and shut the door. And they struck the men who were at the doorway of the house with blindness, both small and great, so that they became weary trying to find the door.*

When the men of Sodom became hostile towards Lot,

the visitors protected Lot by striking the men closest to the doorway with blindness.

> *Then the men said to Lot, "Have you anyone else here? Son-in-law, your sons, your daughters, and whomever you have in the city—take them out of this place! For we will destroy this place, because the outcry against them has grown great before the face of the LORD, and the LORD has sent us to destroy it."*
>
> *So Lot went out and spoke to his sons-in-law, who had married his daughters, and said, "Get up, get out of this place; for the LORD will destroy this city!" But to his sons-in-law he seemed to be joking.*
>
> *When the morning dawned, the angels urged Lot to hurry, saying, "Arise, take your wife and your two daughters who are here, lest you be consumed in the punishment of the city." And while he lingered, the men took hold of his hand, his wife's hand, and the hands of his two daughters, the LORD being merciful to him, and they brought him out and set him outside the city.*

The visitors proclaimed that Sodom would be destroyed and instructed Lot to warn his family. Lot's sons-in-law failed to take him seriously. Lot himself lingered and had to be physically pulled out of the city by the two visitors. Lot and his family were rescued from their giant purely by God's mercy.

Giants Must Die

Sometimes, a giant will simply be too big for you and God will remove you from the situation, like He did for Lot. But more often than not, you will have to fight the giant—not to disarm him or defeat him, but to kill him. Giants do not take neutral ground; they come for what's yours. You need to fight for the things that are yours, the things God has given you. God has given you peace of mind; He has given you joy that the world could never give you. Don't allow any worldly giant to come and take it away.

WORKBOOK

Chapter Ten Questions

Question: Identify some giants in your life. Remember these are not strongholds, built on wrong thinking, but enemies to your soul in the form of temptation or spiritual attack and oppression.

_____

_____

_____

_____

_____

_____

_____

_____

_____

_____

Question: What spiritual and earthly blessings has God given to you, specifically, that are vulnerable to attack by a giant?

_____

_____

_____

_____

_____

_____

_____

_____

_____

_____

_____

Action: Have you ever tried to accommodate rather than defeat a giant? Read examples of people in Scripture who took this approach. For example: the Israelites with the heathen nations around them (Judges 1–2); Saul with the Amalekites (1 Samuel 15); David with his lust for Bathsheba (2 Samuel 11); Pilate at Jesus' trial (Matthew 27); Peter with the legalists (Galatians 2). What new dangers and problems are created by accommodation?

Chapter Ten Notes

CHAPTER ELEVEN

Shriveling Giants

Perhaps you were afraid of the dark when you were a child. Remember how that fear evaporated when your mom turned on the light? The light revealed that all the goblins and bogeymen you had imagined simply weren't there. In the same way, the giant in your life begins to shrink when you stop looking at him and focus on God.

The Israelites went out to do battle against the Philistines, but once they heard Goliath run his mouth and saw how imposing he looked, they turned tail and fled (1 Samuel 17:4–11). They had come to fight, but instead, they ran.

Sometimes we start to take a stand, but when things get serious, we back off because we're scared. We don't face the giant because of our fear. I will admit that the giant is big. I will admit that the giant is loud. But he has nothing on the God who is holding you up and protecting you. If you don't confront and kill the giant, he will continue to hang around, feeding your fear more than your faith.

In 2 Kings, we learn that the King of Syria was warring against Israel and the prophet Elisha kept foiling his attacks. The King of Syria was determined to stop Elisha.

Therefore he sent horses and chariots and a great army there, and they came by night and surrounded the city. And when the servant of the man of God arose early and went out, there was an army, surrounding the city with horses and chariots. And his servant said to him, "Alas, my master! What shall we do?"

So he answered, "Do not fear, for those who are with us are more than those who are with them." And Elisha prayed, and said, "LORD, I pray, open his eyes that he may see." Then the LORD opened the eyes of the young man, and he saw. And behold, the mountain was full of horses and chariots of fire all around Elisha. So when the Syrians came down to him, Elisha prayed to the LORD, and said, "Strike this people, I pray, with blindness." And He struck them with blindness according to the word of Elisha.
—2 Kings 6:14–18

You have the same kind of power at your disposal. If God has called you into battle, He will not allow you to be beaten. You will still have to fight, but He will be right by your side with unseen but powerful hosts to protect you.

God Gives Us Power

God has not left us powerless regarding the works of the Devil. He has extended His authority to us, and He wants us to use it.

And when He had called His twelve disciples to Him, He gave them power over unclean spirits, to cast them out, and to heal all kinds of sickness and all kinds of disease.
—Matthew 10:1

But there are some things in your life that God expects you to beat on your own. Victory will still be accomplished through God's power and strength and with Him by your side. However, when faced with certain kinds of situations, you don't need to wait for God's special intervention to know how to proceed.

If your giant tempts you to hop into bed with people you aren't married to, keep yourself far from situations that may lead you there. If your giant encourages you to gossip and speak ill of people, rebuke your tongue and keep your mouth shut.

You know how I stopped drinking? I learned how convenience stores are set up. I figured out what side my soda was on, and I stopped walking on the side of the store where they sold the alcohol. If there was an alcohol display in one of the aisles, I didn't walk down that aisle.

Budweiser was not going to stop being sold at convenience stores. Miller Light was not going to stop being sold at convenience stores. I had to understand that I could walk into a place that sells alcohol and still go about my business, still be a believer, because God has given me the authority to topple my giant.

God Will Provide

You may wonder if God realizes that you're fighting,

if He understands how tough the battle is. He does, which is why He provides for you as you fight. David is again a good example for us.

> *And the Philistine [Goliath] drew near and presented himself forty days, morning and evening.*
>
> *Then Jesse said to his son David, "Take now for your brothers an ephah of this dried grain and these ten loaves, and run to your brothers at the camp. And carry these ten cheeses to the captain of their thousand, and see how your brothers fare, and bring back news of them."*
> *—1 Samuel 17:16–18*

David's father wanted news from the battle, so he sent David with provisions for his brothers. God is not going to let you battle against the Devil and not give you power, not give you purpose, not give you a reason to defeat that enemy, even though you may be scarred and battle-weary.

Your giant might not be bothering you today, but you might see fellow believers struggling against their giants. God wants you to help them, too.

Say you have people in the church who are battling sexual sin, who sincerely desire to defeat this giant. Other believers often bring them down because they're fornicating.

But guess what? They need help and encouragement to kill their giant. Hurtful criticism and censure only drive them away from God and His people, so the people struggling with sin have little chance of overcoming. If you don't help them and encourage them, all you're doing is giving them more reason to participate in the thing from which they want to be delivered.

The reason I've shared about my struggle with alcohol is because I want you to know that God can deliver a drinker. I want to provide confirmation of God's power so that people who are facing their own giants will be encouraged. If I can be victorious, *you can be victorious.*

The Real Deal

Have you ever gone into a store and seen a product marked "For Display Only"? That means you can't buy the product because it doesn't work the way it's supposed to. Some believers have all the bells and whistles, but that's all it is—a public display.

> *By this all will know that you are My disciples, if you have love for one another.*
> *—John 13:35*

As believers, there's a way that we live, a way that we talk, a way that we walk, that identifies us as belonging to Jesus. We are not just on display; we are the real deal. But if you're just for show, it'll show.

Imagine you arrive at an outdoor basketball court to play a game with some friends. One of the guys shows up dressed in top of the line gear, with everything matching. He walks up with a swagger and begins to make a big display of his stretching. You and the rest of your friends look at each other as if to say, *"Is he serious?"* Throughout the game, it becomes abundantly clear that your friend has no idea how to play basketball—he was just for show.

I've seen plenty of believers who look pretty but perform pitifully. I'm convinced that they dress up so that they have an excuse not to fight. They have their good clothes on, you know, and their mothers would be upset if they got them dirty.

You don't want to be charging into battles without exercising discernment; not every battle is one you're called to fight. But it should be clear to the enemy that you can walk your talk and that if God calls you into battle, you will finish what you started.

If you do not read the Bible regularly and invest time in building your relationship with God, you will lose every battle you fight. I encourage you to take a cue from David. His private prayer life formed the foundation for his public life as a military leader and a ruler. He wrote numerous psalms that express his devotion to God and process the difficulties of life in the context of his relationship with God. Even when David struggled with sin, his private devotional life made it possible for him to repent and get back into step with God.

Jesus is the ultimate example of how a strong private devotional life can influence your public life. In Matthew 4, before Jesus even begins His public ministry, He uses His knowledge of Scripture and His understanding of God's character to put the enemy in his place.

Then Jesus was led up by the Spirit into the wilderness to be tempted by the devil. And when He had fasted forty days and forty nights, afterward He was hungry. Now when the tempter came to Him, he said, "If You are the Son of God, command that these stones become bread." But He answered and said, "It is written, 'Man shall not live by bread alone, but by every word that proceeds from the mouth of God.'"

Then the devil took Him up into the holy city, set Him on the pinnacle of the temple, and said to Him, "If You are the Son of God, throw Yourself down. For it is written: 'He shall give His angels charge over you,' and, 'In their hands they shall bear you up, lest you dash your foot against a stone.'" Jesus said to him, "It is written again, 'You shall not tempt the LORD your God.'"

Again, the devil took Him up on an exceedingly high mountain, and showed Him all the kingdoms of the world and their glory. And he said to Him, "All these things I will give You if You will fall down and worship me." Then Jesus said to him, "Away with you, Satan! For it is written, 'You shall worship the LORD your God, and Him only you shall serve.'"

Then the devil left Him, and behold, angels came and ministered to Him.

—Matthew 4:1–11

Jesus did not re-bind the Devil. He did not tell the Devil to get behind Him. He responded to every lie of the enemy with the truth of Scripture, stripping those lies of their power. But if you don't know what's in the Bible, you don't know how to fight the good fight of faith. If the only portion of the Bible you get are the verses that are read during the church service, you will not be able to defeat the giants in your life.

Without that private devotional life, you will be a public disappointment. Take Peter, for example. He told Jesus, "Even if I have to die with You, I will not deny You!" (Matthew 26:35). He even cut off a man's ear in the Garden of Gethsemane, in an attempt to defend Jesus

(John 18:10).

But once Peter was out in public on his own, everything fell apart.

Having arrested Him, they led Him and brought Him into the high priest's house. But Peter followed at a distance. Now when they had kindled a fire in the midst of the courtyard and sat down together, Peter sat among them. And a certain servant girl, seeing him as he sat by the fire, looked intently at him and said, "This man was also with Him." But he denied Him, saying, "Woman, I do not know Him."

And after a little while another saw him and said, "You also are of them." But Peter said, "Man, I am not!"

Then after about an hour had passed, another confidently affirmed, saying, "Surely this fellow also was with Him, for he is a Galilean." But Peter said, "Man, I do not know what you are saying!"

Immediately, while he was still speaking, the rooster crowed. And the Lord turned and looked at Peter. Then Peter remembered the word of the Lord, how He had said to him, "Before the rooster crows, you will deny Me three times." So Peter went out and wept bitterly.
—Luke 22:54–62

Loving Jesus means standing up for Him when He is attacked by others around you. That kind of love only develops by spending time with Him and coming to know Him intimately. If you don't have a private devotional life, you'll let people talk down about God because you're afraid of what they might say or how they might think of you if you call them out for their foolish talk. Your fear of man will eclipse your love for God.

I don't mean to start trouble, but when I hear people

speaking badly about God, I can't help speaking up. Because I spend time with God privately, there's no way I can stay silent when people start maligning Him in front of me. They don't have to like the God I serve, but I won't stand to hear Him spoken of like that.

Some people are surprised at how strong my reaction is, and they tell me that they didn't mean to offend me. My response is strong because they are talking about someone I spend private time with, and He's nothing like their perception of Him. And I'm not going to let them attempt to deceive others into believing that whoever they're talking about is the God I know and serve. I speak out and defend the true nature and character of God because I know Him.

Not everyone who says to Me, "Lord, Lord," shall enter the kingdom of heaven, but he who does the will of My Father in heaven. Many will say to Me in that day, "Lord, Lord, have we not prophesied in Your name, cast out demons in Your name, and done many wonders in Your name?" And then I will declare to them, "I never knew you; depart from Me, you who practice lawlessness!"
—Matthew 7:21–23

If you do not know God, you are not the real deal. You will not take a stand for Him when it counts. And because you don't know God, God will not know you, either. However, if you devote your life to knowing God, He will give you power and authority over the giants in your life—they will shrivel before your eyes.

WORKBOOK

Chapter Eleven Questions

Question: How do you typically respond when you see others battling their own giants? Why should you get involved? How can you speak the truth in love to someone who is in a spiritual battle or who needs to engage in one?

_____

_____

_____

_____

_____

_____

_____

_____

_____

_____

Question: Do you have regular devotional time with God? How do prayer and the Word help you in overcoming temptation? What scriptures have you memorized? How do you respond when someone maligns the Lord's character?

_____

_____

_____

_____

_____

_____

_____

_____

_____

_____

_____

Action: Read the following verses about power: 2 Timothy 1:7, 1 John 4:4, Ephesians 3:14–21. Which one most speaks to you about God's power available to you? Write or print it out, begin to memorize it, and place it where you will see it often.

Chapter Eleven Notes

CHAPTER TWELVE

Why Fight?

Everyone should be fighting their giants, but not everyone chooses to. When you decide you're going to confront something that everybody should be fighting but isn't, you need to be prepared for people to question your decision.

This happened to David when he visited the Israelites' camp. He heard Goliath's threats and asked what was being done about him

> *Now Eliab his oldest brother heard when he spoke to the men; and Eliab's anger was aroused against David, and he said, "Why did you come down here? And with whom have you left those few sheep in the wilderness? I know your pride and the insolence of your heart, for you have come down to see the battle." And David said, "What have I done now? Is there not a cause?"*
> **—1 Samuel 17:28–29**

Some people are too scared to take initiative, so the

giant continues to hang around. Saul's army was just skulking about, waiting for someone else to volunteer. Meanwhile, Goliath came out every morning to taunt them. Until David showed up.

With David, it was his own brother who spoke badly about David's intention to fight Goliath. This wasn't some random soldier accusing David of pride and insolence—it was his own flesh and blood. Talk about being misunderstood!

Despite his brother's accusations, David had the right response to Goliath's taunts. He got mad, and he decided he was going to shut that giant up. There was no way he was going to put up with Goliath's arrogance and lies, "For who is this uncircumcised Philistine, that he should defy the armies of the living God?" (1 Samuel 17:26). And he was indignant at his brothers for standing around and doing nothing.

I've seen people in the church actually get mad when someone else finally deals with a giant that they themselves should've beaten a long time ago. Far too often, people will allow demons to linger around them indefinitely—until someone realizes the power that God has given us. Little children, the handicapped, and fatherless families call out the sympathies of sensitive Christians.

You may respond to the pain the giant causes, even if it is not your own. If a giant calls you out, you need to fight him, knowing that God has given you power over every giant the Devil brings your way. If people get angry when you display God's power in a situation like this, ignore them. You cannot waste your time and energy worrying about what people think about you when you're fighting giants. When you choose to fight a giant and succeed, you become a target for all those who chose not to fight. They realize that they could've beaten the giants in their lives, too. And some people don't like to be reminded of that.

And God is able to make all grace abound toward you, that you, always having all sufficiency in all things, may have an abundance for every good work.
—2 Corinthians 9:8

Since God is able to make all grace abound toward you, that giant can be as tall as he wants—there is no mountain high enough and no valley deep enough to keep God away. Past victories remind you that He will keep you from being a present victim. Reflect on your life and remember what God has done for you. He has preserved your life, He has kept you from falling, and He is still presenting you faultless (Jude 1:24).

Lions and Bears

When David told Saul that he would fight Goliath, he didn't have any past military victories. But he had similar experiences that had prepared him for this battle.

And Saul said to David, "You are not able to go against this Philistine to fight with him; for you are a youth, and he a man of war from his youth."

But David said to Saul, "Your servant used to keep his father's sheep, and when a lion or a bear came and took a

> lamb out of the flock, I went out after it and struck it, and delivered the lamb from its mouth; and when it arose against me, I caught it by its beard, and struck and killed it. Your servant has killed both lion and bear; and this uncircumcised Philistine will be like one of them, seeing he has defied the armies of the living God." Moreover David said, "The LORD, who delivered me from the paw of the lion and from the paw of the bear, He will deliver me from the hand of this Philistine."
>
> **—1 Samuel 17:33–37a**

David knew about things that can kill and destroy. He knew what it was like to have something precious and valuable snatched away from him, and he knew what it was like to have to fight to get it back.

With God's power, David was able to fight off a bear and lion to keep them from reaching the sheep he guarded.

When I consider many marriages today, I see them torn apart as if they have been attacked by wild animals The Bible says of marriage, "what God has joined together, let not man separate" (Matthew 19:6). If your marriage is troubled, hang on to it. Don't let the wild animal tear it apart and don't let man separate it either. God can keep you together. When the giants of infidelity come, when the giants of mistrust and divorce move in, defend that marriage with all your strength, and God will make you immovable.

It took great courage and extraordinary strength for David to defeat those animals. He was only a teenager at the time. He knew he could never have defeated those wild animals without God's help. So he was confident God would enable him to kill Goliath. And that is the point. If God did it for others, He will do it for you.

The Bible is clear: "Do not touch My anointed ones, and do My prophets no harm" (1 Chronicles 16:22). This is not just a verse for pastors. This is a verse for all believers.

Your past tells you that you will always be victorious. Remember what the Lord has delivered you from and remember that it was He who delivered you. You didn't get here because you somehow mustered up enough strength.

"If it had not been the LORD who was on our side" (Psalm 124:1), where in the world would you be? Probably torn apart by a bear or suffocated by a lion.

"Jesus Christ is the same yesterday, today, and forever" (Hebrews 13:8). He delivered you before, and He will do it again.

Be Who You Are, Do What You Do

When Saul realized that David really was going to fight Goliath no matter what Saul said, he tried to give David his own armor. It didn't quite work out:

So Saul clothed David with his armor, and he put a bronze helmet on his head; he also clothed him with a coat of mail. David fastened his sword to his armor and tried to walk, for he had not tested them. And David said to Saul, "I cannot walk with these, for I have not tested them." So David took them off.

Then he took his staff in his hand; and he chose for himself five smooth stones from the brook, and put them in a shepherd's bag, in a pouch which he had, and his sling was in his hand. And he drew near to the Philistine.
—1 Samuel 17:38–40

Stop trying to be someone else to fight giants. God made you unique, and He has equipped you to fight in your own way. You'll never win the battle saddled with someone else's ill-fitting armor and sword. You don't have to be anyone other than who you are, who God made you to be.

Did God make you physically attractive or very strong? Or are you plain and less than a Samson?

Did He give you the means to dress nicely or drive a nice car? Perhaps you drive a run-down vehicle.

These are all surface issues that mean nothing in the Kingdom. Neither do you need to be a hermit or take a vow of poverty to receive God's power and grace.

So the Philistine came, and began drawing near to David, and the man who bore the shield went before him. And when the Philistine looked about and saw David, he disdained him; for he was only a youth, ruddy and good-looking. So the Philistine said to David, "Am I a dog, that you come to me with sticks?" And the Philistine cursed David by his gods. And the Philistine said to David, "Come to me, and I will give your flesh to the birds of the air and the beasts of the field!"

Then David said to the Philistine, "You come to me with a sword, with a spear, and with a javelin. But I come to you in the name of the LORD of hosts, the God of the armies of Israel, whom you have defied. This day the LORD will deliver you into my hand, and I will strike you and take your head from you. And this day I will give the carcasses of the camp of the Philistines to the birds of the air and the wild beasts of the earth, that all the earth may know that there is a God in Israel. Then all this assembly shall know that the LORD does not save with sword and spear; for the battle is the LORD's, and He will give you into our hands."
—1 Samuel 17:41–47

David knew he didn't have to be Saul or Eliab or Abinadab or Shammah to defeat Goliath, because he knew that he wasn't the one fighting—God was. Because God was in the fight, God would win the fight. Goliath could mock, but David would be himself and fight the way God had made him to fight.

Goliath was probably not impressed by David's choice of weapons, either. In fact, Goliath was likely embarrassed to even fight him. How would it look for the mighty Goliath to defeat a kid like David? It certainly wouldn't earn him any bragging rights. He knew nothing of the power behind that stone in David's hand. But when that stone was mighty through God, it toppled a giant.

So it was, when the Philistine arose and came and drew near to meet David, that David hurried and ran toward the army to meet the Philistine. Then David put his hand in his bag and took out a stone; and he slung it and struck the Philistine in his forehead, so that the stone sank into his forehead, and he fell on his face to the earth. So David prevailed over the Philistine with a sling and a stone, and struck the Philistine and killed him. But there was no sword in the hand of David. Therefore David ran and stood over the Philistine, took his sword and drew it out of its sheath and killed him, and cut off his head with it. And when the Philistines saw that their champion was dead, they fled.

—1 Samuel 17:48–51

Reclaim Your Belongings

Come to Me, all you who labor and are heavy laden, and I will give you rest. Take My yoke upon you and learn from Me, for I am gentle and lowly in heart, and you will find rest for your souls. For My yoke is easy and My burden is light."

—Matthew 11:28–30

What are you giving up to a giant? One of my favorite TV shows is *The Dog Whisperer,* in which Cesar Millan helps families with disobedient dogs causing problems in their households. He likes to say that he rehabilitates dogs, but he trains people.[7]

From watching this show, I learned that when you have a powerful breed of dog as a pet, that dog lives by one law—take possession. You must be strong enough to continually remind the dog that everything in that house belongs to you. If the dog is lying on the couch and growling at you, you need to be the one to tell the dog that you own that couch and he does not. When owners implement Cesar's advice, it is a paradigm shift; it creates a whole new atmosphere in the home.

Do your utmost to change the atmosphere in your life. Reclaim the peace and victory that Jesus won for you on the cross. When you no longer need to consume all your energy fighting for survival, you can take on all the things you have been longing to do for the Kingdom of God.

Chapter Twelve Questions

Question: Why do those with undefeated giants often re-
act negatively toward those who take on their own giants?
Describe a time when you watched someone else get victory in an area where you had not even attempted to fight.
What was your attitude toward that person?

_____

_____

_____

_____

_____

_____

_____

_____

_____

_____

_____

Question: Describe a time when you tried to "wear Saul's armor"—to experience spiritual victory by imitating someone else instead of being who God made you to be, living in His calling for you. What was the result, and how can you learn from that experience?

_____

_____

_____

_____

_____

_____

_____

_____

_____

_____

_____

Action: *When you no longer need to consume all your energy fighting for survival, you can take on all the things you have been longing to do for the Kingdom of God.* Make a list of things that you would like to do or feel a calling to do for God's kingdom. What battles stand between you and those dreams? Ask God to free you from strongholds and giants and to give you strength and victory in the spiritual battles necessary to move on to be a mighty warrior for Him.

Chapter Twelve Notes

CONCLUSION

A Call to Victory

Father, I stretch my hands to thee. No other help I know.
If thou withdraw thyself from me, oh, whither shall I go?[8]
—Charles Wesley

Goliath, in his arrogance said, "Choose a man for yourselves, and let him come down to me" (1 Samuel 17:8). What a powerful verse. Goliath told the Israelites to send a man to fight him, and when Goliath saw David "he disdained him; for he was *only* a youth" (1 Samuel 17:42). The enemy misunderstood who David was. Goliath was looking for a man in stature, but David was a man full of the Spirit of God.

If you do not see yourself the way God sees you, you will never be able to conquer the giant looming over you. God says in His Word that you are "more than [a conqueror] through Him who loved [you]" (Romans 8:37). So that giant that's clouding your mind—kill it today.

God is offering you a full life, but you won't experience it if you allow the enemy to build up strongholds, erect walls, and send giants after you. Having read this book, I hope you feel more prepared for the different kinds of spiritual battles you, as a believer, need to face.

Strongholds are thoughts and ideas that are built upon false beliefs and fester in your mind. They are sometimes hard to identify, but once you know what they are, you don't need to fear facing them. Always remember that, if you are in Christ, He has already won the victory for you. You can rely on the guidance of the Holy Spirit.

Satan uses strongholds to disrupt a believer's walk with God, so it is vital that you recognize them. Of course, it is even better if you can prevent the enemy from building up strongholds in your mind in the first place. Be vigilant at all times and allow other believers whom you respect to speak truth into your life and challenge you.

Whether a particular stronghold is related to the foundations of your faith, or a different area of your life, you can destroy them by leaning on the truth of Scripture and being prayerful, having put on the spiritual armor described in Ephesians 6. Tear down strongholds by taking control of your thought life and being obedient to the Bible.

Walls can be positive or negative, depending on what they are confining and what they are keeping out. The walls you need to tear down are the ones that isolate you from God and His people. These walls protect selfish thoughts and keep the Lord out. Satan loves to use walls to hinder your relationship with God.

Walls can keep you from seeing God, which will lead you to think of yourself as the center of your world. However, just like you can destroy strongholds with God's help, you can tear down walls by following God's battle plan, patiently waiting on Him, and trusting in Him to deliver you.

Unlike strongholds and walls—which remain where they are—giants follow you, challenging you and refusing to back down. Giants make you deal with them, whether you want to or not. It is important to remember that giants are not undefeatable but can be defeated through God's strength.

To be ready for battle, you need to immerse yourself in Scripture and invest time in building a strong relationship with the Lord. To win spiritual battles, you need to have the right perspective, keeping your eyes on the Lord instead of yourself. Jesus, in His unfailing love for you, won the victory for you on the cross. If you remain in Him, relying on Him for everything and giving Him the glory, you will be victorious!

What are you going to do? Make a commitment today. You have God's provision and the testimonies of the past. You can ignore the enemies and the naysayers of the present, be who God made you to be, and turn to Him for help.

If you call on God, He will answer you, and He will show you great and mighty things (Jeremiah 33:3). Call on Him, and experience victory in the battles you are fighting within.

About the Author

Bishop Anthony Pelt is a native Floridian who earned his B.A. in Political Science and his Master's in Public Administration at the University of Central Florida. An ordained bishop, he is the Founding Senior Pastor of Radiant Living Worship Center.

Bishop Pelt has served on several local, state, and international boards, including Youth and Christian Education, Seminary Board of Theology, and the General Assembly Cabinet for the Church of God.

Bishop Pelt is a man who truly loves the Lord, serves the Lord with gladness, and is committed to implementing solid biblical teaching in ministry—to elevate the people in everyday living outside of the church walls with strong belief that "Christian Education is the key to Church Elevation for the total man."

Bishop Pelt has preached throughout the States, Canada, and the Caribbean Islands.

Bishop Pelt has implemented several annual evangelism outreach events, including Community Day, at which free health screenings, Blood Bank Mobile, Mammogram Mobile, a clothing drive, prayer, and food are provided. This event normally serves over 200 people.

Christmas in Grenada, another of these evangelism outreach opportunities, involves purchasing items like shoes and clothing for over 250 children. These items are shipped to Grenada to provide Christmas for needy children. Bishop Pelt also supports the Angel Tree project for kids in the community whose parents are incarcerated.

He has also implemented Man-Up Monday, when men from all around the community come together to share and encourage one another in dealing with any issues they may face.

Bishop Pelt is a community activist and serves as a voice of reason for many people and groups throughout the community. Because of his passion for education and evangelism, he has now adopted the county schools in his city to provide school supplies, book bags, tissues, and hand sanitizers for students who are less fortunate. He also provides a petty cash fund for the local elementary schools to ensure that no child goes without eating at school.

He currently serves as Chairman of the Deerfield Beach Housing Authority. He is a volunteer chaplain for the Broward County Sheriff's Office, a volunteer for Broward County Public Schools, and a guest speaker and mentor for the Jim Moran Youth Automotive Training Center in Deerfield Beach, Florida. He is the past president of the Deerfield Beach Christian Ministerial Association.

Bishop Pelt was recently appointed by the Church of God International Headquarters as the Administrative Bishop for Florida-Cocoa.

He is married to Millicent and has three children—Imani, Tyrone, and Hope.

About Sermon To Book

SermonToBook.com began with a simple belief: that sermons should be touching lives, *not* collecting dust. That's why we turn sermons into high-quality books that are accessible to people all over the globe.

Turning your sermon series into a book exposes more people to God's Word, better equips you for counseling, accelerates future sermon prep, adds credibility to your ministry, and even helps make ends meet during tight times.

John 21:25 tells us that the world itself couldn't contain the books that would be written about the work of Jesus Christ. Our mission is to try anyway. Because in heaven, there will no longer be a need for sermons or books. Our time is now.

If God so leads you, we'd love to work with you on your sermon or sermon series.

Visit www.sermontobook.com to learn more.

REFERENCES

Notes

[1] Strong, James. "G3794 – ochyrōma." In *Strong's Exhaustive Concordance of the Bible* (Hunt & Eaton, 1894), quoted in Blue Letter Bible. https://www.blueletterbible.org/lang/lexicon/lexicon.cfm?Strongs=G3794&t=KJV.

[2] Strong, "G4752 – strateia," in *Strong's Exhaustive Concordance of the Bible* (Hunt & Eaton, 1894), quoted in Blue Letter Bible. https://www.blueletterbible.org/lang/lexicon/lexicon.cfm?Strongs=G4752&t=KJV.

[3] Shriner, Will, dir. *My Wife and Kids.* Season 2, episode 20, "Papa Said Knock You Out." Written by Damien Dante Wayans. Aired February 27, 2002, on ABC.

[4] Durante, Joseph M. "The Roman Weapon: The Legion Armaments." War History Online. December 25, 2017. https://www.warhistoryonline.com/instant-articles/the-roman-weapon.html.

[5] "Groupthink." Merriam-Webster. https://www.merriam-webster.com/dictionary/groupthink.

[6] Galbraith, Deane. "How Tall Was André the Giant Compared to Goliath?" Remnant of Giants. https://remnantofgiants.wordpress.com/2013/10/04/andre-the-giant-versus-goliath.

[7] Millan, Cesar and Melissa Jo Peltier . *Cesar's Rules: Your Way to Train a Well-Behaved Dog.* Crown Archetype, 2010.

[8] Wesley, Charles. "Father, I Stretch My Hands to Thee." In Hymnary.org. https://hymnary.org/text/father_i_stretch_my_hands_to_thee.

Made in the USA
Columbia, SC
28 February 2020

88487140R00083